AF335063

Gallery Books
Editor: Peter Fallon

FUSELAGE

Justin Quinn

FUSELAGE

Gallery Books

Fuselage
is first published
simultaneously in paperback
and in a clothbound edition
on 24 October 2002.

The Gallery Press
Loughcrew
Oldcastle
County Meath
Ireland

ISBN 1 85235 329 5 (*paperback*)
      1 85235 330 9 (*clothbound*)

A CIP catalogue record for this book
is available from the British Library.

The Gallery Press acknowledges the financial assistance
of An Chomhairle Ealaíon / The Arts Council, Ireland,
and the Arts Council of Northern Ireland.

Contents

PART ONE
  Laurel *page* 13

PART TWO
  'Suddenly small islands . . .' 19
  'The thick dark current . . .' 20
  'Our heads drop down . . .' 21
  'Of dreamworks through the rooms . . .' 22
  'Today the State Exams . . .' 23
  'You meet them at mid-afternoon receptions . . .' 24
  'Withhold the name . . .' 26
  'Of ash, of alphabets . . .' 27
  'Observe the sky: it changes . . .' 28
  'Mountains like sentinels . . .' 30
  'Lift the remote control . . .' 32
  'Recently illiteracy . . .' 33
  'Personal history irrelevant . . .' 35
  'The stepping up . . .' 37
  'More or less intact . . .' 38
  'Flashes, specks . . .' 39
  'Fly into London Stansted . . .' 42
  'Three columns stand in massive space . . .' 43
  'Which get the go-by from the Thames . . .' 44
  'A kind of elegance . . .' 45
  'We eat at Rez's . . .' 46
  'The black room on a higher floor . . .' 47
  'And, Jesus, get me out of here . . .' 48
  'Go through and down the steps . . .' 49
  'The two eyes watch . . .' 50
  'They are for commerce . . .' 52
  'Each moment has less force . . .' 53
  'Linger, tag, let go . . .' 54
  'So flood the place with light . . .' 55
  'I wake early into . . .' 56
  'They stand around . . .' 59

Notes and Acknowledgements 61

for Evan Rail

PART ONE

Laurel

1

We sit in the apartment, evening light
still blue and red though it's now getting late.
Summer weather is suddenly upon us,
a sort of strange, extraordinary bonus.
This whole long winter's ice is edged and shoved
away and off and down some twisting shaft —
the awful cold, those months and days and hours,
two heads locked into darkness, mine and yours,
as we moved round the streets, then travelled home
to cook and talk, the central-heating's hum
throughout the honeycomb of our new block.
The almond and viburnum blossoms bulk
so heavily upon the trees, in crowds,
jostling, swaying, rallying against the grades
of gust and breeze. One week, and they unfold
themselves into the city's open vault.
Such widespread fragrance. Gathering of small joy.
The shock. And then a feeling of nostalgia
that sweetens, swells and spreads out through the air,
through both of us.

2

                    Who got up from his chair
and walked out the door to catch a bus or plane?
And who sat here and told us of her plan
to lift her life out of the cooling ashes?

Who was it wished to know the local issues
but couldn't understand the answers, who
brought our son a horse of wood which he
then stood beside his bed when going to sleep?
What were the barbs and laughs, the drift and spiel
that traded back and forth across our board?
They surged and gathered. Then they disappeared.

3

I keep an eye on the world on quiet mornings.
The clouds drift by like mountainous meringues.
The brown apartment buildings list and store
their dreaming hundreds who have yet to stir.
The kestrels bicker back and forth across
the rooftops. Somewhere the noise of crows.
In waves and waves the mixed reports come in.
(It's often best to leave the TV on.)
They eddy through us, lifting up our limbs
into their panorama — swirls and gleams
of rapid imagery and breaking news,
a pageantry, a kind of global nous.
Our bodies join and move in these transactions,
round and round, in antique, practised accents
of want and give, go round in blazon heat
of necessary conjunction, and push ahead
into the open — building, making, saying:
Once upon a time the old Gods sang
Of bodies chang'd to various forms and airs,
Of seasons ceding, making up the years,
Of human creatures risen from the stones
Up into seeing how the sky extends

And dreaming of some muddy origin
That flicker'd from the Gods or in a gene
And gave its tenour to everything that teems,
Deduc'd from Nature's birth to present times.
I love the way our bodies fold around
and into one another, seethe and rend,
then lastly, hurriedly, break out in all joy:
one tiny fleck from off first things, nostalgia
for the love gods have for human form
that generates a further likeness, firm
of limb and mind that wholly takes our love
and lives, before we have to take our leave —
the children echoing down the passages.
The massive pattern increments and edges.
And then it drops us back in things,
a zone that has been emptied of all tidings.
A slight dawn chill though June is almost here.
The earth will warm up as the sun climbs higher.
The vacant chairs. The dishes in the sink.

4

About when I was twenty (you are saying),
I was on my way home up Strahov hill,
going through the park, a kind of hall
of different trees in blossom, and suddenly
it was all too much for me: I had to lie
down on the grass beneath the glinting sun
and feel it in me, as if I had been sown
into the earth and rooted like a tree
before I stretched up skywards, sure and true,
and stayed there swaying in that scene,
forever in love with the only sun.

PART TWO

S UDDENLY SMALL islands
of colour can be seen
through drizzle on the screen —
with fury and in silence

thousands of words and signs
exchanged in the transaction,
eddying. Then one black zone
is flesh and flowing violence:

so beautiful the skin,
so starved and yet so silken —
shimmering with software,

curved and coursing, worth
so much. Press pause just there.
Two eyes watch the earth.

THE THICK dark current runs,
flows out from us — a murmur
ceaseless, full of rumour,
data and vast funds.

The surface coils and rends
itself so monstrously —
swirls flicker strenuously,
then sink like sodden fronds,

as though beneath the surface
something huge had woken —
lazy, moving, limber —

for seconds, and now swerves
off sideways and back down
again into light slumber.

OUR HEADS drop down into the ebb and flash
of all the world. Here is a house and here
the beds held up against our blood and flesh
by campaigns, drives, the sponsoring unclear.
Here is the swift uncoupling of bone
from the choreography of the waking head;
for these dark hours it might as well be stone,
the brain ungrasped, the eyes let go by heed.
Thus folded back into the mesh, we three
lie stockstill through the night — my wife the odd time
wakes, our son rolls round occasionally,
but otherwise unmoved, unmoving:
                                    trireme
with all its oars at rest, the gentle wash
of waves on the hull. Here is the ebb and flash . . .

OF DREAMWORKS through the rooms of this old house
which stands forth in the city's silent hours
(the odd car changing gears, the gnawing mouse)
and has done for the last four hundred years,
itself a complex congeries of dreams,
revisions and repatternings, rebuilt
and rearranged so many times it seems
to slightly float, to flow, to give and tilt
within the greater tilt and give and flow
of Prague at large through black and gold and red —
so many millions packed into its felloe
and swung through centuries, so many dead
who added facets to the ebb and flash
and faded into what they came from: ash.

TODAY THE State Exams. Hour after hour
I tested knowledge . . . no, say rather, power.

Say rather, the necessary information.
How Marlowe died. And who was William Shakespeare.

A protocol for each interrogation.
'Debriefing' for each tired interrogator.

The Cold War is an adequate distraction
from land and sky, from their essential torpor.

The leaves all rushed back into character
as I went out. And then a sudden downpour.

Up on the hill Hradčany *caput mortuum* —
its palaces and spires, its prison tower.

The Pentecostal fire of Marx and Engels
which once enflamed the just and raised the poor

become so many million pilot lights
and briefly Palach, his own funeral pyre.

Because the words are sealed until the last
we go our ways and end for instance here.

Y O U   M E E T them at mid-afternoon receptions
where they have come from their small offices
in ministries. They smile and they profess
an interest in the IMF and options,

anxious to present the facts they know,
yet curious if they feel that you know more,
as if the market and the trading-floor
had been invented just two months ago.

Their ties: diagonals of blue and white
designed a year after the tanks came in,
a sense of speed imparted by flecks of brown;
their shirts the colour of collective wheat;

their smiling tolerance of the dissidents
who now hold power, like parents who indulge
idealistic children and won't divulge
hard truths just yet, their sympathy immense;

their bonhomie; their polished anecdotes —
all this suggests you couldn't have them shot
and afterwards feel good about it, not
because you like the golden Jakeš quotes

(you do) but because they impersonate
a human being oh so well; will even
take out photographs of faded children
(who seem improbable in build and trait).

What they won't mention: X years back the period
when in the role of high apparachiks
they suddenly found that three or so rough weeks
and their Socialist Republic had disappeared,

much as when in a crowded tram you find
your wallet gone, the banknotes and IDs
spirited away by murderers and thieves,
and other dirty bastards of that kind.

WITHHOLD THE name.
Who turns his body whole into a relic,
who turns in flame.

Like wildfire, shame
spreads everywhere — the country is a stalag.
Withhold the name

because its fame
is chaos and strange joy, a wedge of Pollock
turned into flame,

and stakes its claim
by opening heads as spring does buds of lilac.
Hold forth his name

into the game
of to-&-fro that's called cold war and, look,
it turns into flame,

and this freeze-frame
is fluent spirit. Ignore the man's wan plaque.
Withhold the name.
Turn to flame.

O F A S H, of alphabets)

        (the twenty-five-needle jack moves through the air

the pleasure of merely circulating)

             (I live in the Marriott Convention Center

float through the rooms, the house)

                 (and the origin? the target group?

Cahuenga Blvd, V domcích)

                    (accruing, augmenting, alerting

you'll find the port in your arm)

                      (press the fucker firmly in

wondrous sights, strange visions)

             (it's OK, there's probably no one watching

I am, the house says)

                    (the air is thick with *what?*

oh, I've had it with this crap)

                 (abruptly filliped out of the loop

float through the city)

                 (eddies, incidents, -versions

a throwback, like *The Times*)

                   (but chivvying forwards

and all the light erasures)

OBSERVE THE sky: it changes
and remains the same. Cope
of cloud manoeuvres, flow
and fusillades of rain.
You fall up through it

endlessly, you never
come upon its edge.
Its flame is various,
is light and luxury
one moment, then sheers off

and leaves the streets and houses
closed and utterly bereft,
their people sunk back down.
Junkies veer and drift
through the concourse of the Metro.

Lodged inside their skulls
are jewels of *Jetzzeit*. Expanse
of joy and mainly power,
'vital, consecrating, celestial,
all things dissolved into

the waves and surges of
an ocean of light'. The world
is spinning fuselage
& swerves & bends & swoops
in answer to our will

though we don't see or know
each other, what spirit
each is of. We flame forth
beautifully, apart;
shimmer, slide and flow.

MOUNTAINS LIKE sentinels. The forest in darkness.
The water catching bits of light.

The celebrations in the valleys,
mostly marriage hymns,

are where the landsmen gather in an innocence
of earth, and pass down words for things

& reasons that they have for killing and being killed.
The wine, the loaves of bread.

The night air that they move through in large circles
cleansed and purified.

This will last another thousand years
nowhere exactly,

but in, say, seven thousand skulls in spate
through streets, the image thrust forth in their roar,

the OB units taking it all in
and sleeving it inside the cyclone,

with sitcoms, talkshows, advertisements,
tacked onto a wall of wheeling wind that's coursed

with bloodlines, filth and currency. I reach
my hand out into this,

the rushing circles of swung air, its roar.
My hand is frozen to the bone by speed.

Blink.
Held up into the quiet morning,

I hear wrens outside, some voices,
and look out at the streets, the fuselage.

Lift the remote control
and angle it into
the systems, the waves. Sinew
the massive pitch and roll

with choice, each tiny tendril
negotiating a menu.
Do you want to continue?
Yes. But what's central

with its assembled rings
of great debates and threats
is always just beyond.

And then you find the wiring's
coloured rivulets
streaming from your hand.

Recently illiteracy, murder and malnourishment
were re-invented; the logo designed so that

these new products will leap out
from the shelves when you wheel down past

to get your week's stuff — books, food, things
to wipe the baby's ass and your own; designed

so that when you lift your hand out through the space,
the very air, of the supermarket that's faceted with choice

you'll feel that this product is for you,
that your personality is best expressed

through its purchase; it's you; you know it too
and ferry it home with the kind of consumer pride

you associate with the 1940s and '50s
when the world was a better place, and Ma

was not your Da in drag (like now)
and men in suits met in high-ceilinged rooms to

say that there are rights, that there are
human rights, and you could look out the window

into the suburban haze and not feel
that any moment your own hands

would swoop down from the skies
with exceptionally intricate weaponry destroying

foliage, cats, schoolchildren, you also,
while voice-overs promise plenitude, the trickle-down

effect, World Bank suits arriving any minute now, they say;
a time when your hand moving through

the air, whatever air that be,
was not what it (lift it up and look) is today.

P ERSONAL HISTORY irrelevant,
his own or who he's walking toward right now.

Moves like a sequence of blank footage
past cars, across the road, onto the verge,

pure instrument of contract,
raising a hand

and reducing a man/woman to something
on the pavement outside an apartment block;

transaction outside the legal channels,
communication concerning

the gravity of a debt or marriage failed;
no response expected.

Seeds the air, the shot, with filaments of
desire, regret, satisfaction, etc, and shapes the way

you look up at the sky and what you feel
even days later, reading the paper

when it flickers in a brief paragraph;
filaments; a path; fill out the questionnaire.

Which the state calls murder, the sudden collapse
of a whole world put together by eyes and ears and hands,

a huge horizon cancelled —
forty banknotes (light, manoeuvrable) changing hands;

subtract one huge horizon
and still the real one stays there more or less intact.

THE STEPPING up, the sudden information, the seed,
the scattering of force

through pens, computer keyboards, paste-up,
the shot, the recoil and reverberation

is all one tiny blazing fleck from off
'the relentless dissolution of forms and commingling of
    identities,

the confounding of specific qualities
into one indeterminate, purely quantitative process',

a serpent — intricate, violent, not wholly uniform —
nowhere and yet gridding everything

below the threshold of what you know and see;
the flows, the systems:

'the crowds swaying like wind-blown grass, a field of flesh
shot through with sudden eddies

of need and gratification';
the flows, the systems

from which a fleck
flies off and flares through millions of wide minds at once.

*The edge of our world is not distant, it does not stretch to
the horizon or down to the depths; its luminous brink, the
twilight edge of the strait space of our lives, is close by us . . .*

MORE OR less intact, spanning the windshield.
Glare. 110 km/h. Mesmeric

the cars' slow movements in and out of lanes or holding
   course:
sect,

a set of common interests swung through space
along the highway's dreaming

at speed and still enmeshed
in roadsigns, traffic systems, the errand and instructions,

getting, spending
(shake hands, speak softly; the drop off, the pick up):

the complete mechanical cabaret, the by-and-large
that filaments the sky with bloodlines, filth and currency;

otherwise bare board
beneath which there's no brink, however close,

no other city.
I change down to fourth while gliding by

the petrol stations, the shopping malls, the billboards,
and exit at the sector with the large machines for living in.

FLASHES, SPECKS: if not men and women crowding fast
    in the streets
what are they?

They flange out far across the special zones, scud
the pavements' edges,

surge and tack this way and that, into the main drag
or trickle through the sidestreets, saunter,

build up and then the sign, spick torrent flowing loose
across the path of columns of stalled cars:

to the sky-hooked eye an immense panorama
of fluidity and ochlocracy —

mostly hair and flurried cloth — which prompts the
    voice-over to say
fabric

(feel the gear-change, the summoned boost,
like a powerful elevator accelerating upwards into

explanation, overview, expanse,
electronic overlay of appropriate statistics,

the pitch, the soothing timbre
assembled by men and women in dark rooms checking
    levels, watching monitors)

of society,
flesh made spectral,

sorted into a flaring, phosphorescing play
of flindered surface.

& I move through this:
air dense with overview and welded into place

by ampersands and copulae,
which reach and hook into the fabric

cladding me
(GAP jeans, NEXT sale shirt,

their 'Made in' tags discreet
white stigmas stitched on inside seams —

China, Indonesia — flashpoints, joint trade,
flouting of . . .

4402 6028 127* ****
the numbers wielded for the purchase,

connecting with the barcodes,
the tiny fibres

furiously knitting me into the flows, the circuits, the systems
as data: nondescript low buildings

bevelled gently into a hillside in Vermont or Meath,
which house

a layered hum of cooling fans and airconditioning,
& a mainframe, hold it in the undulant landscape,

its dreaming, its sleepless sorting of
the figures coming in from Europe and East Asia)

& make
a massive rippling arras of the world,

of these streets crowded fast:
buoyancy, lift

myriad shuttling motions,
billowing array of coloured stitchwork. Facets

glint here, are grazed matt there, but largely
shimmer, slide and flow.

Fly into London Stansted early.
Friday morning. Commuter train —
it crawls. Worse than the trip from Orly.
Stuffed full of people. Outside, rain.
Jesus, London's such a hole
is what I think in Tottenham Hale.
The undulating boredom, brick
on brick of it. Again the brake,
the pause, the silence. We look out.
The micro-crackle of strip-lighting . . .
Then gears jolt and engage. We're gliding,
gaining speed, the roll, the rocket-
ing. Then suddenly sashaying
into Liverpool Street Station.

THREE COLUMNS stand in massive space.
I queue for half an hour and climb
to a postmodern state of grace.
My self, that whining, small 'I am',
is suddenly grand spectacle
and huge with power. Below, crowds speckle
the sloping concourse of the Tate,
as tiny as statistics (brisk trade
in revelation at the weekend).
I sway above their milling swarms
like Nelson weathering all storms,
as they move round the shops, the sequined
cash-points, corporate logos, the teachers,
the posters, the theories, the great T-shirts.

Wʜɪᴄʜ ɢᴇᴛ the go-by from the Thames.
Southwark, Waterloo — the streets
deserted by their week-day temps,
the multinational ziggurats
slumbering lightly, and Starbucks shut.
The beautiful designs abut
the deeper blacks and blitzkrieged browns
of some place local. An old lush clowns
at the bar of our Holiday Inn,
then comes up to us, flicking her hair:
'I hate you tourists . . . I *live* here.
Just *fuck* off home.' Which is Dublin
for Jack, Stockholm Shane, and Prague
myself. Two days and no jet-lag.

A KIND of elegance . . . almost
balletic as they beat the shit
out of the two slack shapes lying all messed
and bloody on the platform. They shout,
'You were out of order, you were.'
The rest of us somewhat demure
in the face of such strength and conviction.
No announcement, no engine kicks in.
Danger billows in the doorways
still gaping open. Then they disperse.
All the other passengers
left staring at the actual place —
the two men getting to their feet —
the lights, the point-blank pitted concrete.

WE EAT at Rez's, Covent Garden,
up-market Italian, but not outré.
Our waiter acts as though he's starred in
some West End hit for which we three
weren't even called in to audition.
But he's OK, and the mussel dish an
amazing mix of delicate tastes.
We tell old stories, mock Jack's waist,
Shane's vanity and my spud haircut.
The digs and banter leave unmentioned
the legal separation. Our ancient
family house going on the market.
Lost in space. Our childhood shrinks,
but flows in coloured hyperlinks.

THE BLACK room on a higher floor.
A man on TV wearing a mask
tells how he's being blackmailed for
photos of him in panties. No Masoch,
yet it's a careful dominatrix
who'd promised him there'd be no tricks
when she pulled out the camera. He pays
with master/slave on Saturdays.
'Poor fucker,' someone whispers softly
behind the soundtrack of his pleas.
7.5 million of these
go stretching outwards from our lofty
look-out on the river. Small rooms,
huge wants — the endless catacombs.

AND, JESUS, get me out of here,
I think as I step on the shuttle.
Just lift me up into the clear . . .
Proximity like some shtetl.
Too much a place beneath it all,
too local . . . There's the final call.
Time to rise into the slipstreams,
attain the matchless civic freedoms
of miles and miles of open sky
(albeit I go steerage). Surge
of jets and suddenly we emerge
into the dazzling sunlight high
above the city. Exhilaration.
Joy of brightness. Clouds like an ocean.

G O T H R O U G H and down the steps
into this low-lit cave with floral vaults,
the waitresses manoeuvring
past people who are also moving
to *Rebirth of the Cool* — its huge bass volts
juddering through the depths,

and sailing over those
a lithe and black soprano melody.
Impossible to get the lyrics
but it's love and *la vie en rose*
that sweetens through the voice — love is the eddy
that floats & swerves & flicks

out rippling through the hips
of this girl bringing me a beer just now.
She barely lingers, midriff bared,
and seems amidst all this so Tao.
And oh how smoothly, quickly, she now slips,
her tight black trousers flared,

back into the flows
and systems of her global clientele,
the press of KOOKAÏ and GAP clothes,
their jet-lagged, blue-chip ironies,
and her flesh taken with their push and swell,
her mouth, her hands, her eyes . . .

I find the bill days later —
the date, the time, my itemized half-litre,
full record of our brief transaction,
a printed chit with till ID,
which is her numbered name relieved of accent —
SARKA 03.

THE TWO eyes watch them all the time, obsessed
that somewhere in some head the smallest worm
of insurrection seethes. They judge, they test,
and they identify its fluent form.

The two eyes follow every turn and fold,
each fillip and retraction, swear and groan
of talk, the tiny aggregations, bold
accumulations, reckonings, lifted, blown

throughout this huge space with its hum of fans,
the ceaseless noise of huge machinery
that shapes and prints and packages and hands
the fabrics out for air delivery

into the slipstreams of the world. No soul,
no thread of who they are snagged in the loom
and yet these branded textiles must control
their hours and days, their width of living room,

which crates their consciousness so that they move
when other people move, two oceans crossed,
inside such different contracts meaning love,
such different structures of desire and cost,

and their slight sheen of sweat glints in the light,
it flickers from the far side of the earth,
it ripples through the cloth, is gone from sight
before you comprehend the complex dearth

and you manoeuvre off until you reach
whatever conversation marks your fame.
Shimmer there. Show largesse in your speech.
Expand yourself beyond the usual frame.

Take pleasure in the exponential growth
of your great self out through the atmospheres,
let your gaze open further and grasp both
the figures, the crowds. How the static clears.

THEY ARE for commerce and they hold out sex
and bread, apartments, videos, meat,
street after street
across the valley-floor for all our sakes.

Billboards stand forth
from roadsides and the gables of large buildings
suggesting how our flesh and blood can fill things
and can fuck things, and all they can't afford.

The river gleams
and winds its way through these diverse arrangements
beneath the cloudless heavens — strange, immense;
and the houses come forth in the sun's good beams.

The day unfolds
and I explain what I know to my son.
Newsprint is swirled and swept off at a run
along the path; the brown leaves move in shoals.

E ACH M O M E N T has less force than does a dream.
And who knows what becomes a statesman's pride
or gathers in the circuitry's great tide —
the city gone in one intricate gleam,
its men and women dead?

The crowds out on the street are passing by
in fluent raging multitudes, a race
that flashes forth in colours, then gives place
to others underneath a lawless sky
and sheathes the wide earth's face.

But as we walk back to our new abode
through winter winds and snow becoming sleet,
the greatness of the world is stretched complete
along the river and the busy side-road
before our wandering feet.

LINGER, TAG, let go
and drift off through the children's furniture,
while I do lighting.
Crowds on a loop, they flow
and gaze considering their future
spent with each beautifully designed bright thing.

Poor Adam Zagajewski
lies on a desk in Swedish translation
in every showroom —
a heavy Polish key
to Åke's fraught life situation.
You're Åsa and I'm Åke, we consume

and money circulates
with new perspectives, skylights on the world
(Relax, *Newsweek*
says IKEA now rates
quite high in labour-standards — word
is that they care what happens in Mozambique).

We yaw and joke and bicker
through this huge warehouse at the edge of Prague.
I make you out
among the garden wicker,
the pots, the outdoor shelving, rag-tag
terracotta objects — just about,

and don't think that I love you,
Åsa, but that you're woven into me,
although I might
be anybody too.
We exit. There's not much that we see.
Our eyes are blinded by the real sunlight.

S O F L O O D the place with light
and have them come out now.
Five lenses capture how
they drift into our sight.

Millions of eyes in one
all see at once what follows.
Data swells and billows
through endless cables, spun

widewise across the screen.
They tenderly draw near.
They kiss. The cameras track.

Crowds rush across the scene;
police in riot gear
then drive them slowly back.

I WAKE early into
the already azure day.
The leaves, still sleeved in dew,
adjust themselves and sway
like tiny tremor-gaugings.
The black rampaging gangs
that flooded to-&-fro
throughout the night in dreams
(in time to passing trams)
linger briefly, then go.

Receding southwards, deep
into the continent,
a goods train threads one steep
green river valley bend
after another. Thunder
slow-fades to faint trundle.
The fields of yellow rape
stretch both ways from the river
to the interior;
they ripple and stand ripe.

Gaze folded into gaze,
flesh into flesh, like forests
risen in a maze.
The earth is widely forced
by myriad points of view.
So many — wakeful, new —
that flock and scintillate,
each with its glint of self,
plying its trade, its sylph
of silver concentrate.

The moving crowds are caught
by different tracts and cameras.
They wander into shot
and join the swelling arras
for a few moments when
they are the people, then
drift out of their bit parts
back into open day.
I spread my arms and pray.
I love how each day starts.

The roots of this tree stretch
to the entrails of the world
for its deep water; they fetch
it up into the curled
leaf waiting at the height
inside the sky's blue heat,
and for the heavy fruit —
stone folded in sweet flesh.
Eyes that see afresh,
in joy, have this dark root.

Set deep within the eye —
desire: its shuttles and warps
furiously multiply.
The overlapping orbs
load tales into the earth
of death and monstrous birth,
of pristine female beauty
relaxed and unconcerned
that all the world is burned
by some god for her body.

For mine. I stand in clay
and slowly I am covered
by my love's glint and play,
who once moved through the covert,
oblivious and free,
joy of a body, fear
of nothing, and first light
gathering everywhere,
before a sudden flare
of day-star. Then my flight.

for Petr Borkovec

THEY STAND around. They reach into the offing
and pull him slowly out into the theatre.
Dragged struggling from the open, crying and coughing,
he feels arms hold him tight, then tighter.
Sunlight fills an endless corridor.
Suddenly all its doors are shut at once.
It starts from here, the video recorder
is focused and the footage runs and runs.
They hold you out into the world and praise
your small fresh body, your full-throated fuss.
Come in to this enclosure of our days
and stay a while and more. Come home to us,
me stockstill missing all the nurse just said,
your mother lying emptied on the bed.

Notes and Acknowledgements

page 20   This poem paraphrases a passage from *As I Lay Dying* by William Faulkner.

page 23   This poem is written for the late Ian Milner, a New Zealander who as an Australian civil servant passed information to the KGB during the 1940s. In 1951, a job was found for him at the Department of English of the Charles University in Prague, where he worked till his retirement. Together with his wife, Jarmila Milnerová, he was a noted translator of Czech poetry into English; among the poets they translated was Vladimír Holan. Jan Palach was a student of the Charles University who died several days after immolating himself in January 1969 in protest against the Comintern invasion of his country in August 1968. The square where the Arts Faculty of the Charles University is situated is named after him. The last couplet of this poem paraphrases Daniel 12:9.

page 24   Miloš Jakeš was the General Secretary of the Central Committee of the Czechoslovak Communist Party from 1981 to 1989, and head of the People's Militia (1987-1989).

page 28   This is indebted to Reginald Shepherd's poem 'Locale' from his collection *Wrong*. The passage quoted is from Ralph Waldo Emerson's 'The Over-Soul'. *Jetzzeit* was glossed by Walter Benjamin as a 'time of now shot through with chips of Messianic time'.

page 30   'The last men blink. What does that mean? *Blink* is related to Middle English *blenchen*, which means deceive, and to *blenken*, *blinken*, which means gleam or glitter. To blink — that means to play up and set up a glittering deception which is then agreed upon as true and valid — with the mutual tacit understanding not to question the set-up. Blinking: the mutual set-up, agreed upon and in the end no longer in need of explicit agreement, of the objective and static surfaces and foreground facets of all things as alone valid and valuable . . . ' — Martin Heidegger *What Is Called Thinking?*, translation by J Glenn Gray.

page 37 The first quotation is from Terry Eagleton and the second from William Gibson.

page 38 The epigraph is translated from the Czech of Michal Ajvaz and is from his novel *Druhé Město*.

page 53 This poem reworks W B Yeats's 'The Rose of the World'.

page 59 The epigraph is from the beginning of the eighth of the *Duino Elegies* by Rainer Maria Rilke. In Stephen Mitchell's translation, this reads as follows: 'With all its eyes the natural world looks out/ into the Open. Only our eyes are turned/ backward, and surround plant, animal, child/ like traps, as they emerge into their freedom.'